OCR Business Studies Revisio

CW00842739

CS Revision Guide

Contents

Revision Notes

Business Activity, marketing and people

1. Introduction to Business:
- **Definition:** Business refers to any organization or individual engaged in commercial, industrial, or professional activities with the aim of making a profit.
- **Primary Sectors:** Involves the extraction of raw materials and natural resources (e.g., agriculture, mining).
- **Secondary Sectors:** Involves the manufacturing and processing of raw materials into finished goods.
- **Tertiary Sectors:** Involves the provision of services, such as retail, finance, and education.

2. Forms of Business Ownership:
- **Sole Proprietor:** Owned and operated by a single individual. Full control but unlimited liability.
- **Partnership:** Joint ownership by two or more individuals. Shared responsibilities and profits, with unlimited liability.
- **Private Limited Company (Ltd):** Separate legal entity with limited liability for shareholders. Ownership through shares, but not publicly traded.
- **Public Limited Company (Plc):** Publicly traded on stock exchanges. Limited liability for shareholders. Ownership through shares.

3. Business Objectives:
- **Profit Maximization:** Focus on increasing profits.
- **Market Share:** Aim to capture a larger portion of the market.
- **Social Responsibility:** Consideration of ethical and social impacts.
- **Survival and Growth:** Ensuring the business's sustainability and expansion.

4. Factors of Production:
- **Land:** Natural resources used in production.
- **Labour:** Human effort and skills in production.
- **Capital:** Tools, machinery, and finance used in production.
- **Enterprise:** Combines land, labour, and capital to produce goods and services.

5. Business Functions:
- **Marketing:** Identifying customer needs, promoting products, and managing distribution.
- **Finance:** Managing financial resources, budgeting, and financial planning.
- **Operations:** Overseeing production processes and efficiency.
- **Human Resources:** Managing personnel, recruitment, and employee development.

6. Business Aims and Stakeholders:
- **Stakeholders:** Individuals or groups with an interest in the success of the business.
- **Internal Stakeholders:** Employees, owners, shareholders.

- **External Stakeholders:** Customers, suppliers, government, community.

7. *Business Ethics and Social Responsibility:*
- **Business Ethics:** Principles and standards that guide business behaviour.
- **Social Responsibility:** Businesses contribute positively to society and the environment.

8. *Technology and Innovation:*
1. **Innovation:** Introducing new ideas, methods, or products.
2. **Invention:** Creating an entirely new product from scratch.
3. **Impact of Technology:** Enhances efficiency, communication, and competitiveness.

Business Ownership and Location:

1. Factors Influencing Business Location:
Proximity to Market:
- **Advantages:** Reduced transportation costs, faster response to market demands.
- **Considerations:** Market accessibility, distribution networks.

Availability of Resources:
- **Advantages:** Access to raw materials, skilled labour, and infrastructure.
- **Considerations:** Assessing local resource availability.

Cost Factors:
- **Advantages:** Lower production costs.
- **Considerations:** Analysing labour, land, and utility costs.

Infrastructure:
- **Advantages:** Efficient transportation, communication, and utilities.
- **Considerations:** Availability and quality of infrastructure.

Government Policies and Incentives:
- **Advantages:** Tax incentives, grants, and favourable business policies.
- **Considerations:** Researching government support and regulations.

2. Globalization and Business Location:
Globalization Impact:
- **Advantages:** Access to global markets, diverse talent pool.
- **Considerations:** Cultural differences, legal and regulatory compliance.

Offshoring and Outsourcing:
- **Offshoring:** Moving business operations to another country.
- **Outsourcing:** Contracting specific tasks to external providers.

3. Business Location Strategies:
Centralization vs. Decentralization:
- **Centralization:** Concentrating operations in a single location.
- **Decentralization:** Distributing operations across multiple locations.

Expansion and Relocation:
- **Factors:** Market growth, cost considerations, changing business needs.
- **Strategies:** Expanding existing facilities or relocating to new areas.

The Workforce in Business:

1. *Human Resource Management (HRM):*
- **Definition:** The strategic approach to managing the organization's most valuable asset - its people.
- **Functions of HRM:**
    - Recruitment and Selection.
    - Training and Development.
    - Performance Management.
    - Employee Relations.
    - Compensation and Benefits.

2. *Recruitment and Selection:*
- **Recruitment:** The process of attracting potential candidates to apply for job positions.
- **Selection:** Choosing the most suitable candidate from the pool of applicants.
- **Methods:** Job advertisements, recruitment agencies, internal promotions.
- **Considerations:** Skills, qualifications, cultural fit, diversity.

3. *Training and Development:*
- **Training:** Providing skills and knowledge to employees for their current roles.
- **Development:** Preparing employees for future roles and responsibilities.
- **Methods:** On-the-job training, workshops, seminars, e-learning.
- **Benefits:** Improved skills, increased job satisfaction, career advancement.

4. *Performance Management:*
- **Goal:** Ensure employees contribute effectively to organizational goals.
- **Components:**
    - Setting Objectives.
    - Regular Feedback.
    - Performance Appraisals.
    - Recognition and Rewards.
- **Benefits:** Motivation, identification of training needs, career development.

5. *Employee Relations:*
- **Focus:** Maintaining positive relationships between employees and the organization.
- **Strategies:**
    - Effective Communication.
    - Grievance Handling.
    - Conflict Resolution.
    - Employee Engagement Initiatives.
- **Benefits:** Higher morale, reduced turnover, increased productivity.

6. *Compensation and Benefits:*
- **Compensation:** Monetary and non-monetary rewards provided to employees.
- **Benefits:** Non-monetary perks such as health insurance, retirement plans, and flexible work schedules.
- **Strategies:** Fair and competitive salaries, performance-based bonuses.

- **Impact:** Attracting and retaining talent, motivation.

7. Flexible Working Arrangements:
- **Telecommuting:** Working remotely from outside the office.
- **Flexitime:** Flexible working hours.
- **Job Sharing:** Two or more employees share responsibilities for a single job.
- **Benefits:** Improved work-life balance, increased job satisfaction.

8. Workplace Diversity:
- **Definition:** Presence of individuals with various characteristics, backgrounds, and perspectives.
- **Benefits:** Enhanced creativity, improved decision-making, better understanding of diverse markets.
- **Challenges:** Communication barriers, potential conflicts, resistance to change.

9. Health and Safety in the Workplace:
- **Importance:** Ensuring a safe and healthy working environment.
- **Responsibilities:** Employers and employees share responsibility for health and safety.
- **Regulations:** Compliance with local health and safety laws and regulations.
- **Initiatives:** Employee training, safety protocols, regular inspections.

Business Organisation:

Forms of Business Organization:

Sole Trader:
- **Definition:** A business owned and operated by a single individual.
- **Advantages:**
  - Full control over decision-making.
  - Simplicity in formation and operation.
- **Disadvantages:**
  - Unlimited personal liability.
  - Limited access to capital.

Partnership:
- **Definition:** A business owned and operated by two or more individuals.
- **Advantages:**
  - Shared responsibilities and expertise.
  - Relatively easy to establish.
- **Disadvantages:**
  - Unlimited personal liability for partners.
  - Potential for conflicts between partners.

Private Limited Company (Ltd):
- **Definition:** A separate legal entity with limited liability for shareholders.
- **Advantages:**
  - Limited liability for shareholders.
  - Easier access to capital compared to sole proprietorship or partnership.
- **Disadvantages:**
  - Restrictions on the transfer of shares.
  - Financial information disclosure requirements.

Public Limited Company (Plc):
- **Definition:** A company whose shares are publicly traded on stock exchanges.
- **Advantages:**
  - Access to significant capital through the sale of shares.
  - Limited liability for shareholders.
- **Disadvantages:**
  - Complex legal requirements and regulatory scrutiny.
  - Dilution of ownership control.

Organizational Structures

Functional Structure:

- **Description:** Departments are divided based on functions (e.g., marketing, finance, operations).
- **Advantages:**
  - Specialization and efficiency within functions.
  - Clear lines of authority and responsibility.
- **Disadvantages:**
  - Limited communication between functions.
  - Can lead to a lack of flexibility.

Divisional Structure:

- **Description:** Departments are organized by products, services, or geographical locations.
- **Advantages:**
  - Improved focus on specific products or markets.
  - Better adaptation to changes in the external environment.
- **Disadvantages:**
  - Duplication of functions across divisions.
  - Potential for conflicts between divisions.

Matrix Structure:

- **Description:** Employees have dual reporting relationships (functional and divisional).
- **Advantages:**
  - Enhanced communication and coordination.
  - Flexibility in resource allocation.
- **Disadvantages:**
  - Complex reporting relationships.
  - Potential for conflicts and power struggles.

Business Expansion

Organic Growth:
- **Definition:** Expansion achieved through internal processes, such as increased sales and market share.
- **Methods:** Product development, market penetration, diversification.

Inorganic Growth:
- **Definition:** Expansion achieved through external means, such as mergers and acquisitions.
- **Advantages:** Rapid growth, access to new markets and technologies.
- **Disadvantages:** Integration challenges, cultural differences.

Business Location

Factors Influencing Location:
- Proximity to Market.
- Availability of Resources.
- Cost Factors.
- Infrastructure.
- Government Policies and Incentives.

Location Strategies:
- Centralization vs. Decentralization.
- Expansion and Relocation.

Franchising

Definition:
- A business model where an individual (franchisee) operates a business using the branding, products, and services of another company (franchisor).

Advantages:
- Established brand recognition.
- Support from the franchisor in terms of training and marketing.

Disadvantages:
- Ongoing fees and royalties to the franchisor.
- Limited flexibility in business operations.

Financial Information and Decision Making

1. Financial Statements:

Profit and Loss Statement:
- **Purpose:** Reports the revenues, costs, and expenses over a specific period.
- **Components:** Revenue, Cost of Goods Sold (COGS), Gross Profit, Operating Expenses, Net Profit.

Balance Sheet:
- **Purpose:** Provides a snapshot of the company's financial position at a specific point in time.
- **Components:** Assets (Current and Non-current), Liabilities (Current and Non-current), Owner's Equity.

Cash Flow Statement:
- **Purpose:** Tracks the cash inflows and outflows during a specific period.
- **Categories:** Operating Activities, Investing Activities, Financing Activities.

2. Ratio Analysis:

Liquidity Ratios:
- **Current Ratio:** Current Assets / Current Liabilities.
- **Quick Ratio (Acid-Test Ratio):** (Current Assets - Inventory) / Current Liabilities.
- **Purpose:** Assessing the company's ability to meet short-term obligations.

Profitability Ratios:
- **Gross Profit Margin:** (Gross Profit / Revenue) x 100.
- **Net Profit Margin:** (Net Profit / Revenue) x 100.
- **Purpose:** Evaluating the company's ability to generate profits.

3. Sources of Finance:

Internal Sources:
- **Retained Earnings:** Profits reinvested in the business.
- **Sale of Assets:** Selling surplus assets for funds.

External Sources:
- **Bank Loans:** Borrowing from financial institutions.
- **Share Issue:** Raising capital by issuing new shares.
- **Bonds and Debentures:** Long-term borrowing through securities.

Business Issues and Influences

1. *Business Environment:*

Definition:
- The business environment refers to the external factors that can impact the operations and decisions of a business.

Components:
- **Internal Environment:** Factors within the organization.
- **External Environment:** Factors outside the organization.

2. *Globalization:*

Definition:
- Globalization refers to the process of increased interconnectedness and interdependence among countries and businesses.

Impacts:
- Access to global markets, increased competition, cultural diversity.

Challenges:
- Cultural differences, legal complexities, and political instability.

4. *Ethics and Social Responsibility:*

Business Ethics:
- **Definition:** Principles and standards guiding ethical behaviour in business.
- **Importance:** Building trust, avoiding legal issues, and maintaining a positive reputation.

Social Responsibility:
- **Definition:** Businesses taking actions to contribute positively to society and the environment.
- **Initiatives:** Environmental sustainability, community engagement, ethical sourcing.

Stakeholders:

Definition:
- Stakeholders are individuals or groups with an interest in the success and activities of a business.

Types:
- Internal Stakeholders (Employees, Owners).
- External Stakeholders (Customers, Suppliers, Government, Community).

Importance:

- Managing relationships with stakeholders is crucial for business success.

The Wider World

1. Globalization:
Definition:
- Globalization is the process of increased interconnectedness and interdependence among countries, economies, and businesses.

Key Features:
- Increased international trade and investment.
- Cultural exchange and diversity.
- Rapid communication and technological advancements.

Impacts:
- Access to new markets, increased competition, and cultural exchange.

2. International Trade:
Benefits:
- Access to a wider market.
- Economic growth and job creation.
- Specialization and efficiency.

Challenges:
- Currency fluctuations, trade barriers, and cultural differences.

3. Multinational Corporations (MNCs):
Definition:
- Multinational corporations are companies that operate in multiple countries, with a centralized home office.

Characteristics:
- Global operations, diverse workforce, and adaptability to local markets.

Impacts:
- Economic development, job creation, and technology transfer.

4. Environmental and Ethical Considerations:

Sustainability:
- Integrating environmentally sustainable practices into business operations.

Ethical Practices:
- Adhering to ethical standards in global business dealings.

The Interdependent Nature of Business

1. Interdependence Definition:
- Interdependence in business refers to the mutual reliance and interconnectedness between different entities, both within and outside the organization.

2. Stakeholders:
- **Definition:** Individuals or groups who have an interest or stake in the activities and success of a business.
- **Examples:** Shareholders, employees, customers, suppliers, government, and the local community.

3. *Internal Interdependence:*

a. Functional Areas:
- Different departments within a business are interdependent.
- Examples: Marketing relies on information from Finance for budgeting.

b. Teams and Employees:
- Collaboration among teams and effective communication is essential.
- Examples: Sales teams depend on product information from the production team.

4. *External Interdependence:*

a. Suppliers:
- Businesses rely on suppliers for the timely and quality provision of raw materials or goods.
- Examples: Manufacturing depends on a stable supply of raw materials.

b. Customers:
- The demand for products or services is driven by customer needs.
- Examples: Retailers are dependent on customer preferences and purchasing power.

5. Financial Interdependence:

a. Creditors and Lenders:
- Businesses may rely on loans or credit from financial institutions.
- Examples: Investment for expansion or working capital loans.

b. Investors:
- Shareholders provide capital in exchange for a share in the company.
- Examples: Businesses may seek funding through share issues.

6. Market Interdependence:

a. Competitors:

- Businesses in the same industry compete for market share.
- Examples: Pricing strategies and product differentiation.

b. Collaboration:
- Businesses may collaborate for mutual benefit.
- Examples: Joint ventures or strategic partnerships.

7. Technological Interdependence:

a. Supply Chain Technology:
- Use of technology to enhance efficiency in the supply chain.
- Examples: Automated inventory systems and online ordering.

b. Information Systems:
- Businesses rely on information systems for data management.
- Examples: Customer relationship management (CRM) systems.

8. *Global Interdependence:*

a. International Trade:
- Businesses operate in a global market with cross-border transactions.
- Examples: Importing/exporting goods and services.

b. Global Supply Chains:
- Businesses source materials globally, creating interdependence.
- Examples: Automotive companies sourcing parts globally.

9. *Environmental Interdependence:*

a. Sustainability:
- Businesses are influenced by environmental concerns.
- Examples: Adoption of sustainable practices for corporate social responsibility.

b. Regulatory Compliance:
- Businesses must adhere to environmental regulations.
- Examples: Waste management and emissions control.

Short Answer Questions

1. **Human Resources:**
   - **Question:** Explain the importance of effective human resource management in meeting the needs of business activity.
   - **Answer:** Effective human resource management ensures that the right people with the necessary skills are recruited and retained, contributing to improved productivity and organizational success.

2. **Financial Resources:**
   - **Question:** Outline the potential consequences for a business with poor financial management.
   - **Answer:** Poor financial management can lead to cash flow issues, financial instability, inability to invest in growth opportunities, and even bankruptcy.

3. **Market Research:**
   - **Question:** Discuss the role of market research in helping businesses identify and meet customer needs.
   - **Answer:** Market research provides insights into customer preferences, market trends, and competitor strategies, enabling businesses to tailor their products or services to meet customer demands effectively.

4. **Innovation and Technology:**
   - **Question:** How can businesses use innovation and technology to gain a competitive advantage?
   - **Answer:** Embracing innovation and technology allows businesses to enhance efficiency, improve products or services, and stay ahead of competitors, ultimately leading to a competitive advantage.

5. **Legal and Regulatory Compliance:**
   - **Question:** Explain why it is crucial for businesses to comply with legal and regulatory requirements.
   - **Answer:** Compliance ensures that businesses operate ethically, avoid legal issues, and build trust with stakeholders, contributing to long-term sustainability.

1. **Physical Resources:**
   - **Question:** Discuss the significance of effective supply chain management in optimizing physical resources for a business.
   - **Answer:** Effective supply chain management ensures timely procurement, efficient inventory control, and minimized wastage, contributing to the optimal utilization of physical resources.

2. **Marketing and Sales:**
   - **Question:** Explain the concept of the marketing mix and how businesses can use it to meet customer needs.
   - **Answer:** The marketing mix includes product, price, place, and promotion. Businesses can use these elements to create a comprehensive strategy that aligns with customer needs and preferences.

3. **Customer Service:**
   - **Question:** Why is excellent customer service crucial for the success of a business, and how does it contribute to meeting customer needs?
   - **Answer:** Excellent customer service enhances customer satisfaction, builds loyalty, and generates positive word-of-mouth, all of which contribute to meeting and exceeding customer needs.

4. **Risk Management:**
   - **Question:** Identify and discuss three types of business risks, and explain how businesses can manage or mitigate them.
   - **Answer:** Types of risks include financial, operational, and strategic. Businesses can manage these risks through financial planning, quality control measures, and contingency planning.

5. **Innovation and Technology:**
   - **Question:** Provide examples of how businesses can incorporate innovation and technology into their operations to improve efficiency.
   - **Answer:** Examples include implementing automation in production processes, adopting advanced data analytics for decision-making, and utilizing online platforms for sales and marketing.

6. **Human Resources:**
   - **Question:** Discuss the role of employee training and development in enhancing the overall performance of a business.
   - **Answer:** Employee training and development improve skills, increase job satisfaction, and contribute to employee retention, ultimately enhancing the business's overall performance.

7. **Financial Resources:**
   - **Question:** Explain the importance of effective budgeting for businesses and how it contributes to financial stability.
   - **Answer:** Effective budgeting helps allocate resources efficiently, set financial goals, and monitor performance, ensuring financial stability and supporting strategic decision-making.

8. **Market Research:**
   - **Question:** Elaborate on the steps involved in conducting market research and how businesses can use the gathered information.
   - **Answer:** Market research involves defining the problem, collecting data, analysing data, and making decisions. Businesses can use this information to identify market opportunities, assess demand, and develop targeted strategies.

9. **Legal and Regulatory Compliance:**
   - **Question:** Discuss the potential consequences for a business that fails to comply with environmental regulations.
   - **Answer:** Non-compliance with environmental regulations can lead to fines, legal actions, damage to the company's reputation, and adverse effects on the environment, impacting the overall sustainability of the business.

10. **Innovation and Technology:**

- **Question:** How can businesses encourage a culture of innovation among employees, and why is it essential for long-term success?
- **Answer:** Businesses can encourage innovation by fostering a supportive environment, promoting collaboration, and providing resources for research and development. Innovation is crucial for adapting to changing markets and staying competitive in the long run.

11.

Practice Questions

12. **1.** *Internal Interdependence:*
13. a. Explain how different functional areas within a business are interdependent.

14. b. Provide examples of internal interdependence between teams and employees.

15. **2.** *External Interdependence:*
16. a. Discuss the importance of suppliers in the external interdependence of a business.

17. b. How does customer demand contribute to external interdependence?

18. **3.** *Financial Interdependence:*
19. a. Describe the role of creditors and lenders in the financial interdependence of businesses.

20. b. How do businesses manage their relationships with investors to ensure financial stability?

21. **4.** *Market Interdependence:*
22. a. Explain how competitors impact the market interdependence of businesses.

23. b. Provide examples of collaboration between businesses to achieve mutual benefits.

24. **5.** *Technological Interdependence:*
25. a. Discuss the role of technology in supply chain management and its impact on technological interdependence.

26. b. How do businesses use information systems to enhance technological interdependence?

27. **6.** *Global Interdependence:*
28. a. Analyse the challenges and opportunities of international trade for businesses in terms of global interdependence.

29. b. Discuss the significance of global supply chains in the interdependent nature of business.

30. **7.** *Environmental Interdependence:*
31. a. Explain how sustainability practices contribute to the environmental interdependence of businesses.

32. b. Discuss the role of regulatory compliance in environmental interdependence.

33. **8.** *Social and Ethical Interdependence:*
34. a. Describe the concept of corporate social responsibility (CSR) and its impact on social interdependence.

35.b. How does change consumer behaviour influence the social and ethical interdependence of businesses?

Sample Answers

1. Internal Interdependence:
a. Functional areas within a business are interdependent as they collaborate to achieve common organizational goals. For example, the finance department provides budget information to the marketing department, enabling effective planning and resource allocation.

b. Teams and employees are interdependent as they rely on each other's expertise and collaboration. For instance, sales teams depend on the product development team for accurate and timely information about new products.

2. External Interdependence:
a. Suppliers play a crucial role in external interdependence by providing raw materials or goods necessary for production. Businesses rely on suppliers for a stable and quality supply chain.

b. Customer demand contributes to external interdependence as businesses must adapt their products and services to meet changing customer preferences and purchasing patterns.

3. Financial Interdependence:
a. Creditors and lenders are essential for financial interdependence as they provide businesses with necessary funds through loans or credit, enabling investment and operations.

b. Businesses manage relationships with investors by providing transparent financial information and ensuring a fair return on investment, contributing to financial stability.

4. Market Interdependence:
a. Competitors impact market interdependence by influencing pricing strategies and product differentiation, shaping the competitive landscape.

b. Collaboration between businesses, such as joint ventures or strategic partnerships, contributes to mutual benefits and shared success in the market.

5. Technological Interdependence:
a. Technology in supply chain management enhances efficiency and coordination among businesses, fostering technological interdependence.

b. Information systems, such as Customer Relationship Management (CRM) systems, are used to streamline communication and enhance technological interdependence.

6. Global Interdependence:
a. International trade presents challenges such as currency fluctuations but also offers opportunities for businesses to access new markets, demonstrating the complexity of global interdependence.

b. Global supply chains facilitate the movement of goods and services across borders, showcasing the significance of global interdependence.

7. *Environmental Interdependence:*
a. Sustainability practices contribute to environmental interdependence by promoting eco-friendly business operations and reducing the ecological impact.

b. Regulatory compliance ensures that businesses adhere to environmental standards, playing a vital role in environmental interdependence.

8. *Social and Ethical Interdependence:*
a. Corporate social responsibility (CSR) impacts social interdependence by fostering ethical business practices and community engagement.

b. Changing consumer behaviour influences businesses to adopt socially responsible and ethical practices, contributing to social and ethical interdependence.

1. *Internal Interdependence:*
a. Explain how effective communication between different functional areas can enhance internal interdependence within a business.

b. Provide examples of situations where internal interdependence between teams is crucial for achieving organizational objectives.

2. *External Interdependence:*
a. Discuss the impact of external interdependence on a business's supply chain and its relationship with suppliers.

b. How does external interdependence with customers influence marketing strategies and product development?

3. *Financial Interdependence:*
a. Explain the role of financial interdependence in the decision-making process when a business seeks external funding.

b. Discuss how businesses balance the interests of creditors and investors in the context of financial interdependence.

4. *Market Interdependence:*
a. Analyse how market interdependence affects pricing strategies and product differentiation among competitors.

b. Provide examples of collaborative initiatives between businesses that demonstrate market interdependence.

5. *Technological Interdependence:*
a. Explore the role of technology in promoting interdependence between different stages of the supply chain.

b. How can information systems contribute to improving technological interdependence within a business?

6. *Global Interdependence:*
a. Evaluate the challenges and benefits of global interdependence for businesses engaged in international trade.

b. Discuss how global supply chains demonstrate the interdependent nature of businesses on a global scale.

7. *Environmental Interdependence:*
a. Explain how businesses can demonstrate environmental interdependence through sustainable practices.

b. Discuss the impact of regulatory compliance on the environmental interdependence of businesses.

8. *Social and Ethical Interdependence:*
a. Explore how corporate social responsibility (CSR) initiatives contribute to social interdependence.

b. Discuss the ethical considerations businesses must navigate, demonstrating ethical interdependence.

Sample Answers

1. *Internal Interdependence:*
a. Effective communication between functional areas ensures a smooth flow of information and resources within a business. For example, when the marketing department communicates with finance, it helps align marketing budgets with overall financial goals.

b. Internal interdependence is crucial in scenarios such as new product development. The marketing team relies on the product development team for accurate information about features and specifications to create compelling marketing campaigns.

2. *External Interdependence:*
a. External interdependence with suppliers is critical for maintaining a stable and efficient supply chain. Businesses depend on suppliers for timely deliveries and quality materials, impacting production schedules.

b. External interdependence with customers influences marketing strategies. By understanding customer preferences, businesses can tailor their products and marketing messages to meet specific demands.

3. *Financial Interdependence:*
a. Financial interdependence plays a significant role when a business seeks external funding. For instance, when securing a loan, businesses must consider the terms offered by creditors and the impact on overall financial stability.

b. Balancing the interests of creditors and investors involves transparent financial reporting. Striking the right balance ensures that both creditors and investors feel confident in the financial health of the business.

4. Market Interdependence:
a. Market interdependence affects pricing strategies and product differentiation. Businesses must monitor competitors' actions to adjust pricing and differentiate their products effectively.

b. Collaborative initiatives between businesses, such as co-branding or co-marketing campaigns, showcase market interdependence. These collaborations aim to expand market reach and share resources.

5. Technological Interdependence:
a. Technology promotes interdependence within the supply chain by enabling real-time communication and data exchange. For example, advanced software allows manufacturers to coordinate with suppliers seamlessly.

b. Information systems contribute to technological interdependence by streamlining internal processes. CRM systems, for instance, enhance communication between sales and customer service teams.

6. Global Interdependence:
a. Global interdependence presents challenges like navigating different legal frameworks, but it also offers benefits such as accessing diverse markets. Businesses engaged in international trade must adapt to global economic dynamics.

b. Global supply chains demonstrate how businesses rely on partners worldwide for components and materials. An interruption in one part of the chain can impact operations globally.

7. Environmental Interdependence:
a. Businesses demonstrating environmental interdependence through sustainable practices contribute to long-term ecological health. Initiatives like reducing carbon footprints and promoting recycling showcase commitment to environmental responsibility.

b. Regulatory compliance is a key aspect of environmental interdependence. Adhering to environmental laws ensures businesses operate ethically and sustainably.

8. Social and Ethical Interdependence:
a. CSR initiatives contribute to social interdependence by addressing community needs. For example, philanthropic activities demonstrate a business's commitment to supporting social causes.

b. Ethical interdependence involves navigating complex ethical considerations in business decisions. Businesses must ensure that their actions align with ethical standards to maintain trust with stakeholders.

6 Mark Questions

Marketing and Sales:

- **Question:** Discuss the importance of effective pricing strategies for businesses. Provide examples and explain how a well-designed pricing strategy can contribute to meeting customer needs.
- **Answer:** An effective pricing strategy is crucial for businesses as it directly impacts customer perception and influences purchasing decisions. For instance, a penetration pricing strategy, where a product is initially priced lower than competitors, can attract price-sensitive customers and gain market share. On the other hand, a premium pricing strategy positions a product as high-quality and exclusive, appealing to customers seeking luxury items.

A well-designed pricing strategy contributes to meeting customer needs by aligning product value with price, thus enhancing customer satisfaction. It also allows businesses to differentiate themselves in the market, cater to specific customer segments, and achieve financial objectives.

Innovation and Technology:

- **Question:** Explain how embracing technological innovation can provide a competitive advantage for businesses. Illustrate your answer with examples of how technology adoption can lead to improved efficiency and market competitiveness.

- **Answer:** Embracing technological innovation offers businesses a competitive advantage by enhancing efficiency and providing unique selling points. For instance, implementing advanced manufacturing technologies, like automation and robotics, can improve production speed and quality. Additionally, adopting data analytics tools allows businesses to gain valuable insights into customer behaviour, enabling personalized marketing strategies.

Technological innovation not only streamlines internal processes but also enables businesses to offer innovative products or services, staying ahead of competitors. This proactive approach to technology adoption contributes to market competitiveness, operational excellence, and overall business success.

Financial Resources:

- **Question:** Explain the significance of financial planning for businesses. Provide examples of financial planning strategies and how they contribute to the overall financial health and sustainability of a business.
- **Answer:** Financial planning is crucial for businesses as it involves setting financial goals, creating budgets, and developing strategies to achieve these goals. For instance, creating a detailed cash flow forecast helps businesses anticipate periods of high and low cash flow, enabling better management of working capital.

Effective financial planning also involves investment decisions, such as choosing between debt and equity financing. For example, a business might opt for long-term loans to fund expansion projects, reducing the risk of overreliance on short-term debt. Overall, financial planning ensures that a business has the necessary funds for day-to-day operations, growth initiatives, and unforeseen circumstances, contributing to financial stability and long-term sustainability.

Human Resources:

- **Question:** Discuss the role of employee motivation in meeting the needs of business activity. Provide examples of motivational strategies that businesses can implement to enhance employee performance and job satisfaction.
- **Answer:** Employee motivation is integral to meeting the needs of business activity as motivated employees are more productive and engaged. Businesses can use various strategies to enhance motivation, such as implementing performance-based incentives like bonuses or recognition programs.

Creating a positive work environment through initiatives like flexible work schedules or employee development programs also contributes to motivation. For instance, providing opportunities for skill enhancement and career advancement can increase job satisfaction and loyalty.

Ultimately, a motivated workforce leads to increased productivity, reduced turnover, and improved overall business performance, aligning with the needs of business activity.

Legal and Regulatory Compliance:

- **Question:** Discuss the importance of legal and regulatory compliance for businesses. Provide examples of regulations that businesses commonly need to comply with and explain how non-compliance can impact the overall operations and reputation of a business.
- **Answer:** Legal and regulatory compliance is crucial for businesses to operate ethically and within the boundaries of the law. Examples of regulations include labour laws, environmental regulations, and data protection laws. Non-compliance can lead to legal actions, fines, and damage to a business's reputation.

For instance, a failure to comply with data protection regulations, such as GDPR, can result in significant fines and a loss of customer trust. Therefore, businesses must invest in compliance measures, such as regular audits and employee training, to avoid legal consequences and maintain a positive reputation in the market.

Physical Resources:

- **Question:** Explain the role of effective supply chain management in optimizing physical resources for businesses. Provide examples of how businesses can enhance their supply chain efficiency to meet customer needs and reduce costs.
- **Answer:** Effective supply chain management is essential for optimizing physical resources in businesses. For example, implementing just-in-time inventory systems minimizes storage costs and reduces waste. Additionally, building strong relationships with reliable suppliers ensures a steady flow of materials.

Streamlining transportation and logistics, such as using technology for route optimization, contributes to faster deliveries and customer satisfaction. By optimizing the supply chain, businesses can meet customer demands promptly, reduce operational costs, and maintain a competitive edge in the market.

Human Resources:

- **Question:** Discuss the impact of effective employee training programs on the overall performance and competitiveness of a business. Provide examples of training methods and explain how they contribute to employee development and organizational success.
- **Answer:** Effective employee training programs significantly impact a business's overall performance and competitiveness. One training method is on-the-job training, where employees learn through hands-on experience. For example, a new sales representative might shadow an experienced colleague to understand customer interactions.

Another method is off-the-job training, such as workshops or external courses. This can enhance employees' skills and knowledge, contributing to improved job performance. For instance, a software development team participating in a coding workshop may acquire new programming techniques.

Employee training contributes to organizational success by increasing productivity and adaptability. Well-trained employees are more efficient in their roles and can adapt to technological advancements. Additionally, training fosters employee satisfaction and loyalty, reducing turnover rates.

In conclusion, investing in effective training programs not only enhances employee skills but also strengthens the business's competitive position by ensuring a skilled and adaptable workforce.

Human Resources

- **Question:** Analyse the impact of a diverse workforce on organizational success. Provide examples of strategies that businesses can adopt to promote diversity and inclusion in the workplace, explaining how these strategies contribute to enhanced performance and innovation.
- **Answer:** A diverse workforce can have a profound impact on organizational success by bringing together individuals with varied backgrounds, experiences, and perspectives. This diversity fosters creativity, innovation, and a broader understanding of customer needs. One strategy to promote diversity is implementing inclusive hiring practices, ensuring fair representation of different demographic groups.

For instance, creating a diverse interview panel and using blind recruitment processes can help eliminate biases. Additionally, businesses can establish diversity training programs to educate employees on the value of diversity and foster an inclusive culture. This inclusivity contributes to improved employee morale and collaboration.

A diverse workforce also enhances problem-solving capabilities and adaptability. When employees from different backgrounds collaborate, they bring a range of solutions to challenges. Another strategy is forming employee resource groups that provide support and networking opportunities for underrepresented groups, fostering a sense of belonging and loyalty.

In conclusion, promoting diversity and inclusion in the workplace through inclusive hiring practices, diversity training, and employee resource groups can lead to a more innovative and successful organization.

Business Ownership and Location:

- **Question:** Discuss the advantages and disadvantages of sole proprietorship as a form of business ownership. Additionally, explain the significance of choosing an appropriate business location and the factors that businesses should consider when selecting a location.
- **Answer:** Sole proprietorship as a form of business ownership has both advantages and disadvantages. One advantage is simplicity in decision-making, as the sole proprietor has full control over the business. Moreover, the owner receives all profits, providing a direct financial incentive. However, a major disadvantage is unlimited liability, exposing the owner's personal assets to business debts.

Choosing an appropriate business location is crucial for success. Accessibility is a key factor, as businesses need to be easily reachable by target customers. For instance, a retail store located in a high-traffic area may attract more customers. Proximity to suppliers and distribution networks is also important for operational efficiency.

Moreover, the local business environment, including taxes and regulations, influences the choice of location. For example, a business might opt for a location with favourable tax policies. Additionally, understanding the demographic characteristics of the area, such as the target market's preferences and buying power, is essential for tailoring products or services to local needs.

In conclusion, while sole proprietorship offers simplicity and direct profit control, it comes with the disadvantage of unlimited liability. Choosing an appropriate business location involves considering factors like accessibility, proximity to suppliers, and the local business environment, all of which significantly impact the business's success.

Business Ownership

- **Question:** Compare and contrast the advantages and disadvantages of a limited company with those of a partnership as forms of business ownership. Additionally, discuss the role of location in the success of a retail business, providing examples of how an effective choice of location can contribute to profitability.
- **Answer:** Limited companies and partnerships are distinct forms of business ownership, each with its own set of advantages and disadvantages. A limited company offers limited liability, separating personal and business assets, which is a significant advantage. However, it involves more complex legal requirements and higher administrative costs compared to a partnership, where the owners share responsibilities but also liabilities.

The choice of location is critical for the success of a retail business. A prime location, such as a bustling shopping district, can significantly enhance visibility and foot traffic, leading to increased sales. For example, a clothing store situated in a popular shopping mall can attract a diverse range of customers.

On the other hand, poor location choices, like areas with low consumer traffic or limited accessibility, can hinder a retail business's performance. For instance, a high-end boutique located in a less affluent neighbourhood may struggle to attract the target market.

In summary, while a limited company provides limited liability but involves greater legal complexities, partnerships offer shared responsibilities but also shared liabilities. For retail businesses, choosing an effective location is crucial for maximizing visibility and attracting the target customer base.

Business Ownership and Location:

- **Question:** Compare and contrast the advantages and disadvantages of a limited company with those of a partnership as forms of business ownership. Additionally, discuss the role of location in the success of a retail business, providing examples of how an effective choice of location can contribute to profitability.
- **Answer:** Limited companies and partnerships are distinct forms of business ownership, each with its own set of advantages and disadvantages. A limited company offers limited liability, separating personal and business assets, which is a significant advantage. However, it involves more complex legal requirements and higher administrative costs compared to a partnership, where the owners share responsibilities but also liabilities.

The choice of location is critical for the success of a retail business. A prime location, such as a bustling shopping district, can significantly enhance visibility and foot traffic, leading to increased sales. For example, a clothing store situated in a popular shopping mall can attract a diverse range of customers.

On the other hand, poor location choices, like areas with low consumer traffic or limited accessibility, can hinder a retail business's performance. For instance, a high-end boutique located in a less affluent neighbourhood may struggle to attract the target market.

In summary, while a limited company provides limited liability but involves greater legal complexities, partnerships offer shared responsibilities but also shared liabilities. For retail businesses, choosing an effective location is crucial for maximizing visibility and attracting the target customer base.

Business Ownership:

- **Question:** Compare and contrast the advantages and disadvantages of a partnership with those of a private limited company as forms of business ownership. Additionally, discuss the importance of a suitable business location for both partnerships and private limited companies, outlining key considerations and providing examples.
- **Answer:** Partnerships and private limited companies represent different structures of business ownership, each with unique characteristics. In a partnership, two or more individuals share responsibilities and liabilities. A private limited company, on the other hand, provides limited liability for its shareholders but may involve more complex administrative processes.

Advantages and Disadvantages:

- *Partnership:* Advantages include shared responsibilities and flexibility, but it comes with unlimited liability. In contrast, a *private limited company* offers limited liability but involves greater legal formalities and potentially higher costs.

Importance of Business Location: Choosing an appropriate location is critical for both partnerships and private limited companies. Accessibility to target markets is vital. For instance, a city-centre location might benefit a partnership of consultants seeking local clients. Alternatively, a private limited company in the manufacturing sector might prioritize proximity to suppliers and transportation hubs for cost-effective logistics.

Consideration of the local business environment is crucial. A partnership may find success in a location with minimal regulatory hurdles, while a private limited company might weigh factors like tax incentives and industry-specific regulations.

Examples:

- A law firm partnership might thrive in a central business district due to its accessibility to clients.
- A private limited company in the tech sector might benefit from a location with proximity to research institutions and skilled workforce.

In conclusion, partnerships and private limited companies have distinct pros and cons. The choice of business location is pivotal, impacting accessibility, costs, and regulatory aspects, ultimately influencing the success of both business structures.

Business Ownership:

- **Question:** Analyse the advantages and disadvantages of a public limited company compared to a sole proprietorship. Additionally, discuss the significance of the business location for a public limited company, outlining key considerations and providing examples.
- **Answer:** Public limited companies and sole proprietorships represent distinct forms of business ownership, each with unique characteristics. A public limited company is owned by shareholders and can trade its shares publicly, while a sole proprietorship is a business owned and operated by a single individual.

Advantages and Disadvantages:

- *Public Limited Company (PLC):* Advantages include access to capital through the sale of shares and limited liability for shareholders. However, disadvantages may include a complex organizational structure and increased regulatory requirements. In contrast, a *Sole Proprietorship* offers simplicity in decision-making but comes with unlimited liability for the owner.

Significance of Business Location: The business location is critical for both public limited companies and sole proprietorships. For a PLC, the choice of location can impact its ability to attract investors and customers. A central business district location may enhance visibility and prestige, attracting both shareholders and clients. However, the costs associated with prime locations need to be considered.

For a sole proprietorship, the choice of location directly affects customer accessibility and competition. For example, a sole proprietor running a local bakery may benefit from a high-traffic location in a residential neighbourhood, attracting walk-in customers. However, the costs of prime locations should be balanced against the potential customer base.

Examples:

- A PLC in the financial sector might choose a prestigious city location for its headquarters to enhance its corporate image.
- A sole proprietorship offering personalized services, such as a boutique consultancy, may thrive in a location with a concentration of businesses seeking such services.

In conclusion, while a PLC offers advantages related to capital and limited liability, a sole proprietorship provides simplicity but with personal liability. The choice of business location is pivotal for both, influencing their visibility, competitiveness, and overall success.

Using and Managing Resources:

- **Question:** Discuss the significance of effective resource management in achieving business objectives. Provide examples of how businesses can efficiently use and manage human resources, ensuring both employee satisfaction and organizational success.
- **Answer:** Effective resource management is crucial for businesses to achieve their objectives efficiently. Human resources, being a key component, play a vital role in this context. Businesses can enhance human resource management in various ways to ensure both employee satisfaction and organizational success.

One approach is through talent acquisition and retention strategies. For example, implementing a comprehensive recruitment process that aligns with the company culture ensures the selection of candidates who fit well within the organization. This, in turn, contributes to a positive work environment and employee satisfaction.

Employee training and development programs are also essential. By investing in ongoing skill development, businesses empower employees to perform at their best, contributing to organizational success. Training programs can cover a range of areas, from technical skills to leadership development.

Moreover, fostering a culture of open communication and providing opportunities for employee feedback promotes a sense of involvement and satisfaction. Businesses can implement regular performance reviews, encourage employee suggestions, and address concerns promptly.

In conclusion, effective resource management, particularly in human resources, is integral to achieving business objectives. Businesses that prioritize talent acquisition, invest in training, and foster open communication create an environment that not only satisfies employees but also contributes significantly to overall organizational success.

Technology

- **Question:** Analyse the role of technology in optimizing the use of physical resources in a manufacturing business. Provide examples of how technological advancements can enhance production efficiency, reduce waste, and contribute to the overall sustainability of the business.
- **Answer:** Technology plays a pivotal role in optimizing the use of physical resources in manufacturing businesses, contributing to enhanced efficiency and sustainability. Several advancements can be highlighted:

1. Automation and Robotics:

- *Example:* Introducing automated machinery and robotics in the production process reduces the reliance on manual labour, leading to increased production speed, precision, and consistency. This not only improves efficiency but also minimizes the risk of human error.

2. Data Analytics for Inventory Management:

- *Example:* Implementing data analytics tools allows businesses to analyse historical demand patterns, enabling more accurate demand forecasting. This, in turn, helps in maintaining optimal inventory levels, reducing excess stock, and minimizing storage costs.

3. Sustainable Manufacturing Technologies:

- *Example:* Utilizing sustainable manufacturing technologies, such as 3D printing with eco-friendly materials or energy-efficient machinery, aligns with environmental concerns. This not only reduces the environmental impact but also enhances the company's reputation in the context of corporate social responsibility.

4. Supply Chain Management Systems:

- *Example:* Implementing advanced supply chain management systems enhances the visibility of the entire supply chain. This allows for better coordination between suppliers and manufacturers, reducing delays and optimizing the use of resources throughout the production process.

In conclusion, the integration of technology in manufacturing businesses contributes significantly to the optimization of physical resources. By embracing automation, data analytics, sustainable technologies, and advanced supply chain management, businesses can enhance efficiency, reduce waste, and align with sustainability goals, ultimately ensuring long-term success.

Human Resource Management

- **Question:** Assess the impact of effective human resource management on the success and competitiveness of a business. Provide examples of human resource strategies and practices that contribute to employee engagement and organizational performance.
- **Answer:** Effective human resource management is pivotal for the success and competitiveness of a business. Several human resource strategies and practices contribute to employee engagement and organizational performance:

1. Recruitment and Selection:

- *Example:* Implementing thorough recruitment and selection processes ensures the hiring of skilled and culturally aligned employees. This leads to a workforce that contributes effectively to organizational goals, enhancing competitiveness.

2. Training and Development:

- *Example:* Investing in continuous training and development programs enhances employees' skills and keeps them abreast of industry trends. This contributes to improved job performance, innovation, and adaptability, fostering organizational success.

3. Performance Management:

- *Example:* Establishing clear performance expectations and providing regular feedback contributes to employee engagement. Performance management practices, such as goal-setting and performance appraisals, align individual efforts with organizational objectives.

Financial Management:

- **Question:** Examine the significance of break-even analysis in guiding financial decisions for businesses. Provide examples of how break-even analysis is applied and explain how it informs decisions related to pricing strategies and cost management.
- **Answer:** Break-even analysis is a crucial tool in financial decision-making for businesses, providing insights into the point at which total revenue equals total costs. This analysis is instrumental in guiding decisions, especially in pricing strategies and cost management.

Application of Break-Even Analysis:

1. **Setting Pricing Strategies:**
   - *Example:* Consider a manufacturing company that produces widgets. By conducting break-even analysis, the company can determine the minimum price per widget required to cover both variable and fixed costs. This helps in setting competitive yet profitable pricing strategies.
   - *Explanation:* Break-even analysis assists businesses in understanding the minimum sales volume needed to cover costs. Pricing above the break-even point contributes to profit, while pricing below it may result in losses. This informs pricing decisions to ensure profitability.
2. **Cost Management and Decision-Making:**
   - *Example:* A service-oriented business conducts break-even analysis to assess the impact of cost changes. If fixed costs increase due to a new facility, the analysis helps in determining the necessary sales volume to offset the higher costs.
   - *Explanation:* Break-even analysis aids in evaluating the sensitivity of the business to cost fluctuations. It guides decisions on cost management by highlighting the volume of sales required to maintain profitability. This informs cost-cutting or efficiency improvement strategies.

In conclusion, break-even analysis is a valuable tool for businesses, informing decisions related to pricing strategies and cost management. By understanding the break-even point, businesses can set optimal prices, manage costs effectively, and make informed decisions that contribute to financial sustainability and success.

Financial Management:

- **Question:** Evaluate the importance of financial forecasting in supporting strategic decisions for businesses. Provide examples of two financial forecasting techniques, explaining how they assist in planning and decision-making processes within an organization.
- **Answer:** Financial forecasting plays a vital role in supporting strategic decisions for businesses by providing insights into future financial performance. Two important financial forecasting techniques are **Cash Flow Forecasting** and **Sales Forecasting.**

1. Cash Flow Forecasting:

- *Example:* A company prepares a monthly cash flow forecast projecting the expected cash inflows and outflows for the upcoming six months. It takes into account factors such as customer payments, supplier payments, and other operational expenses.
- *Importance:* Cash flow forecasting is critical for planning liquidity and ensuring that the business has enough cash to cover its operational needs. It aids in decision-making by highlighting potential cash shortages or excesses, enabling proactive measures like securing additional funding or optimizing cash management.

2. Sales Forecasting:

- *Example:* A retail business uses historical sales data, market trends, and seasonality patterns to project future sales for different product categories over the next year. This forecast informs production planning and inventory management.
- *Importance:* Sales forecasting is essential for decision-making related to production levels, inventory management, and overall business strategy. By anticipating changes in demand, businesses can adjust their operational plans, marketing strategies, and resource allocation to align with expected sales volumes.

In conclusion, financial forecasting, exemplified by cash flow forecasting and sales forecasting, is crucial for supporting strategic decisions. These techniques provide valuable insights into future financial conditions, enabling businesses to plan effectively, allocate resources efficiently, and make informed decisions that contribute to long-term success.

Globalisation:

- **Question:** Analyse the impact of global economic factors on businesses. Provide examples of specific global economic influences and discuss how businesses can navigate challenges and capitalize on opportunities in the global market.
- **Answer:** Global economic factors exert a significant influence on businesses, shaping their strategies, challenges, and opportunities. Several specific influences highlight this impact:

1. Exchange Rates and Currency Fluctuations:

- *Example:* Changes in exchange rates can affect the cost of importing raw materials or exporting finished goods. For instance, a strengthening of the home currency may increase production costs for businesses relying on imported materials.
- *Impact:* Businesses need to navigate currency fluctuations by employing effective hedging strategies, pricing adjustments, and diversifying suppliers or markets. Adapting to exchange rate dynamics is crucial for maintaining competitiveness in the global market.

2. Global Supply Chain Disruptions:

- *Example:* Events like natural disasters, political unrest, or a global health crisis can disrupt global supply chains. For example, the COVID-19 pandemic led to widespread disruptions, affecting the availability of raw materials and finished products.
- *Impact:* Businesses must develop resilient supply chain strategies, incorporating risk management and diversification. This involves identifying alternative suppliers, adopting digital technologies for real-time tracking, and implementing contingency plans to mitigate disruptions.

3. Trade Policies and Tariffs:

- *Example:* Changes in trade policies and the imposition of tariffs, as seen in international trade tensions, can impact the cost of importing and exporting goods. For instance, increased tariffs may raise production costs for businesses relying on global supply chains.
- *Impact:* Businesses need to stay informed about evolving trade policies and explore opportunities in emerging markets. Diversifying markets, understanding trade regulations, and advocating for favourable policies are strategies to navigate challenges and capitalize on global opportunities.

In conclusion, global economic factors pose both challenges and opportunities for businesses. Navigating these influences requires strategic adaptability, risk management, and proactive measures to capitalize on the potential benefits of participating in the global marketplace.

Influences on Business:

- **Question:** Evaluate the impact of environmental sustainability considerations on businesses. Provide examples of how businesses can incorporate sustainable practices into their operations and discuss the potential benefits and challenges associated with adopting environmentally friendly strategies.
- **Answer:** Environmental sustainability considerations have become increasingly important for businesses, influencing their strategies and operations. Several examples highlight the incorporation of sustainable practices:

1. Renewable Energy Adoption:

- *Example:* Businesses can invest in renewable energy sources, such as solar or wind power, to reduce reliance on non-renewable energy. This not only lowers carbon emissions but also contributes to long-term cost savings.
- *Benefits and Challenges:* The benefits include a reduced environmental footprint, positive brand image, and potential cost savings in the long run. However, challenges may include initial investment costs, regulatory compliance, and the need for technological adjustments.

2. Sustainable Supply Chain Practices:

- *Example:* Businesses can adopt sustainable sourcing practices, such as using ethically produced raw materials or supporting fair trade initiatives. This ensures social and environmental responsibility throughout the supply chain.
- *Benefits and Challenges:* The benefits encompass improved corporate social responsibility, enhanced brand reputation, and alignment with consumer preferences. Challenges may involve identifying sustainable suppliers, potential cost implications, and the need for effective communication about these practices.

3. Waste Reduction and Recycling:

- *Example:* Businesses can implement waste reduction strategies and promote recycling within their operations. This may include minimizing single-use plastics, encouraging recycling programs, and adopting circular economy principles.
- *Benefits and Challenges:* The benefits include reduced environmental impact, cost savings through efficient resource use, and positive customer perception. Challenges may involve the need for infrastructure investment, employee training, and navigating complex waste management regulations.

In conclusion, incorporating environmental sustainability into business operations is essential for long-term success. While businesses stand to gain numerous benefits, including positive brand image and potential cost savings, challenges exist in terms of initial investments, regulatory compliance, and adapting to new practices. However, the overall impact on the environment and society makes the pursuit of sustainability a crucial aspect of modern business strategy.

Influences on Business:

- **Question:** Examine the impact of changing consumer preferences on businesses. Provide examples of how businesses can respond to shifting consumer trends and discuss the potential benefits and challenges associated with adapting to evolving customer demands.
- **Answer:** Changing consumer preferences significantly impact businesses, necessitating strategic responses to remain competitive. Here are examples of how businesses can respond and the associated benefits and challenges:

1. E-commerce Integration:

- *Example:* Businesses can adapt to the growing preference for online shopping by enhancing their e-commerce platforms, providing a seamless online shopping experience, and investing in digital marketing.
- *Benefits and Challenges:* The benefits include reaching a broader audience, increased convenience for customers, and potential cost savings. Challenges may involve initial investment in technology, addressing cybersecurity concerns, and navigating increased competition in the online space.

2. Sustainable Product Offerings:

- *Example:* Responding to consumers' increasing focus on sustainability, businesses can introduce environmentally friendly and ethically sourced products, promoting a commitment to social and environmental responsibility.
- *Benefits and Challenges:* Benefits include attracting environmentally conscious consumers, enhancing brand reputation, and contributing to global sustainability efforts. Challenges may involve higher production costs, the need for supply chain adjustments, and effectively communicating the sustainability aspects to consumers.

3. Personalization and Customization:

- *Example:* Businesses can respond to the demand for personalized experiences by offering customizable products, tailored services, and personalized marketing communications based on customer preferences and behaviours.
- *Benefits and Challenges:* Benefits include improved customer loyalty, increased customer satisfaction, and the ability to charge premium prices for personalized offerings. Challenges may include data privacy concerns, the need for advanced data analytics capabilities, and maintaining efficiency in production processes.

In conclusion, businesses need to adapt to changing consumer preferences to remain relevant and competitive. While responding to evolving trends offers numerous benefits, including increased customer loyalty and expanded market reach, challenges may include initial investments, operational adjustments, and navigating potential risks associated with new strategies.

Globalisation:

- **Question:** Assess the impact of global economic events on a specific industry of your choice. Provide examples of how a global economic event has influenced the industry, discuss the strategies businesses within the industry have employed to mitigate challenges, and analyse the potential long-term implications for the industry.
- **Answer:** The impact of global economic events on industries is profound, influencing operations, strategies, and long-term prospects. Let's consider the impact of the global economic recession of 2008 on the automotive industry.

Global Economic Event:

- *Example:* The 2008 global economic recession led to a significant decline in consumer spending, particularly on non-essential items such as automobiles.

Impact on the Automotive Industry:

- *Examples:* Sales of new cars plummeted as consumers prioritized essential expenses. Automotive manufacturers faced financial strain, excess inventory, and reduced profitability.

Strategies Employed by the Automotive Industry:

- *Examples:*
  1. **Cost-Cutting Measures:** Many manufacturers implemented cost-cutting strategies, such as layoffs, production cuts, and renegotiating supplier contracts, to reduce operational expenses.
  2. **Shift to Fuel-Efficient Models:** Some companies shifted focus to producing fuel-efficient and smaller vehicles to align with changing consumer preferences and regulatory trends.
  3. **Diversification and Global Expansion:** To mitigate reliance on a single market, some manufacturers diversified their geographical presence, entering emerging markets with growth potential.

Long-Term Implications for the Automotive Industry:

- *Analysis:* While the industry recovered over time, the recession prompted a shift in consumer preferences towards fuel efficiency, sustainability, and technological innovation. This led to long-term changes in the industry, with a greater emphasis on electric and hybrid vehicles, advanced safety features, and digital connectivity.

In conclusion, the 2008 global economic recession had a profound impact on the automotive industry, necessitating strategic responses for survival and growth. The industry's adaptability to changing consumer demands and global economic conditions has resulted in a transformed landscape with a focus on sustainability and innovation.

Marketing and Enterprise:

- **Question:** Analyse the role of digital marketing in promoting entrepreneurial ventures. Provide examples of specific digital marketing strategies, discuss how they contribute to brand awareness and customer engagement, and evaluate the potential challenges and benefits for entrepreneurs.
- **Answer:** Digital marketing plays a pivotal role in promoting entrepreneurial ventures, leveraging online channels to reach and engage target audiences. Let's explore this in more detail:

Digital Marketing Strategies for Entrepreneurial Ventures:

- *Examples:*
  1. **Social Media Marketing:** Utilizing platforms like Instagram, Facebook, and Twitter to create brand awareness, share engaging content, and interact with the target audience.
  2. **Search Engine Optimization (SEO):** Optimizing online content to improve its visibility on search engines, ensuring that the entrepreneurial venture is easily discoverable by potential customers.
  3. **Email Marketing:** Sending targeted and personalized emails to build relationships with customers, share updates, and promote products or services.

Contribution to Brand Awareness and Customer Engagement:

- *Examples:*
  1. **Social Media Engagement:** Regular posts, interactions, and user-generated content on social media platforms contribute to increased brand visibility and engagement.
  2. **SEO and Website Visibility:** Effective SEO enhances the online presence, making the entrepreneurial venture more visible to individuals actively searching for relevant products or services.
  3. **Email Campaigns:** Well-crafted email campaigns can inform customers about new offerings, promotions, or updates, fostering ongoing engagement.

Potential Challenges and Benefits for Entrepreneurs:

- *Challenges:*
  1. **Resource Constraints:** Entrepreneurs may face budget limitations for comprehensive digital marketing campaigns.
  2. **Algorithm Changes:** Platforms frequently update algorithms, impacting the visibility of content and requiring entrepreneurs to adapt strategies.
  3. **Data Privacy Concerns:** Increasing concerns about data privacy may affect the effectiveness of targeted digital marketing efforts.
- *Benefits:*
  1. **Cost-Effectiveness:** Compared to traditional marketing, digital marketing often offers more cost-effective channels for entrepreneurs.
  2. **Global Reach:** Digital marketing allows entrepreneurs to reach a global audience, expanding market potential.

3. **Measurable Results:** Digital marketing provides tools for tracking and analysing performance, enabling entrepreneurs to adjust strategies based on real-time data.

In conclusion, the strategic use of digital marketing is essential for entrepreneurial ventures. While it offers numerous benefits, entrepreneurs must navigate challenges such as resource constraints and evolving platform algorithms to maximize the impact of their digital marketing efforts.

Marketing:

- **Question:** Assess the impact of digital marketing trends on the promotional activities of businesses. Provide examples of recent digital marketing trends, discuss how businesses can leverage these trends to enhance promotional strategies, and analyse the potential advantages and challenges associated with the adoption of digital marketing in today's business landscape.
- **Answer:** Digital marketing trends play a crucial role in shaping promotional activities for businesses. Let's explore the impact of recent trends, examples, advantages, challenges, and an analysis of their adoption:

Recent Digital Marketing Trends:

- *Examples:*
    1. **Video Marketing:** Businesses are increasingly using short-form videos on platforms like TikTok and Instagram Reels to engage audiences.
    2. **Influencer Collaborations:** Leveraging influencers on various social media platforms to reach and resonate with target audiences.
    3. **Chatbots and AI:** Implementation of chatbots on websites and AI-driven personalized messaging for customer interaction.

Advantages of Digital Marketing Trends:

- *Examples:*
    1. **Increased Engagement:** Video content and interactive formats boost audience engagement and sharing.
    2. **Targeted Communication:** Influencer marketing enables businesses to reach specific demographics with authentic recommendations.
    3. **Efficiency and Personalization:** Chatbots provide instant responses, enhancing customer experience through personalized interactions.

Challenges of Digital Marketing Trends:

- *Examples:*
    1. **Saturation and Competition:** Growing competition in digital spaces may lead to content saturation, making it challenging for businesses to stand out.
    2. **Authenticity Concerns:** Maintaining authenticity in influencer collaborations is crucial to building and retaining trust.
    3. **Technology Dependence:** Businesses need to keep up with evolving technologies, which may require investments in training and infrastructure.

Analysis of Adoption Impact:

- *Analysis:* Adopting recent digital marketing trends offers businesses opportunities for increased visibility, engagement, and personalized communication with their audience. However, challenges such as maintaining authenticity, dealing with content saturation, and staying technologically updated require strategic planning and adaptability.

In conclusion, embracing recent digital marketing trends is essential for businesses to stay relevant and competitive in today's dynamic landscape. The effective utilization of these trends can lead to enhanced promotional strategies and improved customer engagement.

Multiple-Choice Practice Questions

1. **Which of the following is a primary function of marketing in a business?**
   a) Human Resources
   b) Financial Management
   c) Operations
   d) Promotion and Sales

2. **What is a key characteristic of a sole trader business structure?**
   a) Limited liability
   b) Separate legal entity
   c) Owned by shareholders
   d) Unlimited liability

3. **What does SWOT analysis stand for in business terms?**
   a) Strengths, Weaknesses, Opportunities, Threats
   b) Sales, Workforce, Operations, Technology
   c) Suppliers, Wage rates, Orders, Taxes
   d) Stock, Warehousing, Orders, Transportation

4. **Which of the following is a component of the marketing mix?**
   a) Leadership
   b) Logistics
   c) Legal Structure
   d) Price

5. **What is the purpose of a balance sheet in financial reporting?**
   a) To record daily transactions
   b) To show a company's financial position at a specific point in time
   c) To track sales and revenue
   d) To analyse market trends

6. **Which type of business organization provides limited liability to its owners?**
   a) Sole trader
   b) Partnership
   c) Private limited company
   d) Public limited company

7. **What is the purpose of a cash flow statement?**
   a) To show a company's financial position at a specific point in time
   b) To analyse market trends
   c) To track the movement of cash in and out of a business
   d) To calculate return on investment

8. **Which economic system relies on supply and demand to determine prices and production levels?**
   a) Socialism
   b) Communism

c) Market economy
d) Command economy

9. **What is a common objective of human resource management in businesses?**
   a) Maximizing profits
   b) Reducing marketing expenses
   c) Attracting and retaining qualified employees
   d) Improving production efficiency

10. **What is the purpose of market segmentation in marketing strategy?**
    a) a) Increase product prices
    b) b) Target specific customer groups
    c) c) Reduce competition
    d) d) Expand distribution channels

11. **Which financial statement shows a company's profitability over a specific period?**
    a) a) Balance sheet
    b) b) Cash flow statement
    c) c) Profit and Loss Account
    d) d) Statement of retained earnings

12. **What does SWOT analysis stand for in a business context?**
    a) Strengths, Weaknesses, Opportunities, Threats
    b) Sales, Workforce, Operations, Technology
    c) Suppliers, Warehousing, Order processing, Transportation
    d) Strategic, Workflow, Objectives, Tasks

13. **What is a key function of human resources in a business?**
    a) Financial planning
    b) Production scheduling
    c) Employee recruitment and management
    d) Market research

14. **What is the purpose of break-even analysis?**
    a) Determine optimal pricing
    b) Assess profitability at different production levels
    c) Evaluate market share
    d) Analyse customer satisfaction

15. **Which form of business ownership offers limited liability to its owners?**
    a) Sole proprietorship
    b) Partnership
    c) Limited liability company (LLC)
    d) Corporation

16. **What is the term for the process of bringing a new product to the market?**
    a) Market research
    b) Product development
    c) Distribution
    d) Market penetration

17. **What is the main purpose of a mission statement in a business?**
   a) Outline specific financial goals
   b) Communicate the organization's purpose and values
   c) Provide detailed operational instructions
   d) Identify short-term objective

18. **In the context of marketing, what does the term "SWOT" represent?**
   a) Sales, Warehouse, Operations, Transportation
   b) Strengths, Weaknesses, Opportunities, Threats
   c) Strategic, Workflow, Objectives, Tasks
   d) Suppliers, Workforce, Order processing, Technology

19. **Which type of market research involves gathering data directly from individuals through surveys, interviews, or focus groups?**
   a) Secondary research
   b) Experimental research
   c) Observational research
   d) Primary research

20. **What financial statement provides a snapshot of a company's financial position at a specific point in time?**
   a) Income statement
   b) Cash flow statement
   c) Statement of retained earnings
   d) Balance sheet

21. **In a business context, what is the purpose of a product life cycle?**
   a) Assessing market share
   b) Analysing distribution channels
   c) Understanding the stages a product goes through from introduction to decline
   d) Setting pricing strategies

Answers:

1. d) Promotion and Sales
2. d) Unlimited liability
3. a) Strengths, Weaknesses, Opportunities, Threats
4. d) Price
5. b) To show a company's financial position at a specific point in time
7. c) Private limited company
8. c) To track the movement of cash in and out of a business
9. c) Attracting and retaining qualified employees
10. b) Set long-term financial goals
12. a) Many sellers
13. c) Employee recruitment and management
14. b) Assess profitability at different production levels
15. c) Limited liability company (LLC)
16. b) Product development
17. b) Communicate the organization's purpose and values
18. b) Strengths, Weaknesses, Opportunities, Threats
19. d) Primary research
20. d) Balance sheet
21. c) Understanding the stages a product goes through from introduction to decline

Printed in Great Britain
by Amazon

40705296R00036